1 INTRODUCTION

Children of all ages take part in many different sports at various levels – from pre-school gymnastics sessions to teenagers competing in national competitions. They take part for many reasons but most of all for fun. This is what sport should be about – having fun. Helping children to take part in sport can be very rewarding. You can gain considerable pleasure and satisfaction from their enjoyment and achievement. This pack will help you get started and apply your effort so you all enjoy yourselves more.

Adults can help children in various ways. Perhaps you are a parent who goes along to support your child as a matter of duty; maybe you are the only one who can drive the minibus to competitions. You might simply enjoy watching a particular game or activity, or want to stay in touch because you were once a competent performer.

What_____ can be_____ are a_____ interest_____ his or_____. If you have driven the team to the practice session, why not ask if you can help, rather than just killing time until the drive home again? If you know a sport well, pass on your knowledge and skill to the next generation of participants. Children need sport and children need skilled leaders to guide them in that sport. *Making Sport Fun* will enable you to become a skilled helper.

Most of all – sport should be fun

Sport has a great deal to offer all children and young people – the talented and the less co-ordinated, the able and those with disabilities. Only however, if it is in the hands of responsible adults who can nurture the positive opportunities and experiences sport can offer.

WHY DO CHILDREN NEED SPORT?

Sport brings adventure, challenge and excitement into children's lives. Taking part helps develop their confidence and self-awareness, and provides a way to release emotions and energy in a controlled environment. In addition, it offers opportunities to work in co-operation with others and to learn about competition.

It provides a way to release emotion and energy

These experiences can contribute to the mental and physical development of children and help them develop some of the skills needed for living in society. However, before getting too carried away with these noble and worthy aspects of sport, remember sport can have a detrimental effect – there are dangers in forcing children beyond their capabilities and interests, and in creating a climate in which winning is seen as everything.

Competition can be of great value in providing the motivation and challenge to strive for a personal goal. It should be used to enhance and develop children's personal performance – not to measure it. In the wrong hands, sport can be very damaging to self-esteem and negative experiences can lead to an aversion to taking part in any sport or physical activity. Remember that above all, sport for young people should provide fun and enjoyment.

WHY DO YOU WANT TO BE INVOLVED?

If you are considering doing more than the bare minimum and want your efforts to be effective, first consider the following questions:

- Why do you want to help?
- Is your main aim to help everyone to win medals?
- How important are fun and enjoyment for you and the children?

As a skilled helper, you may be responsible for influencing the attitudes and lives of your performers both in and out of sport, so it is essential that your own motivation and commitment are genuine and well thought out.

WHAT DO CHILDREN WANT FROM YOU?

Essentially children need your guidance and respect. This means getting to know the sport but more importantly, getting to know children of all ages. It is surprisingly easy to know just a few in a very narrow age-band or social group and to assume all the others are broadly similar. They are not – they come in two sexes and a variety of sizes, colours, backgrounds and abilities.

They do not all develop at the same rate – some may be physically well developed for their age but emotionally quite immature; some may be socially adept while others may lack the social skills normally expected of children of their age. You need to recognise and respect their differences and try to understand each one.

You should be positive and give them encouragement and support, so you can help them all to make the most of their abilities.

WHAT IS YOUR ROLE?

As a helper in sport, you can play many roles:

- As *guardian,* you are there to ensure enjoyable and safe play (Section 3 Page 5).
- As *organiser,* you must ensure every child gets the maximum opportunity and time in each session to enjoy his or her sport (Section 4 Page 13).
- As *motivator,* your concern is with generating a positive and responsible approach in each child (Sections 5–7 Pages 15–26).
- As *teacher,* your role is to impart new knowledge and skills at the right pace and at the appropriate time (Sections 6–7 Pages 19–26).
- As *trainer,* you are concerned with improving the children's health and physical fitness and also their readiness and ability to participate in sport (Section 8 Page 27).

Children come in a variety of sizes, colours, backgrounds and abilities

WHAT DO YOU NEED TO KNOW?

The more you know, the better you will be able to help. However, you do not have to be an expert – you simply have to be prepared to learn and to recognise the common sense safety requirements. If there is a coach attached to the group, ask for advice on how you can fit into the sessions most effectively. If there is no coach, this pack will help you get started and should encourage you to develop the skills to become a coach (further details on Page 30).

You do not have to be a technical expert to help children enjoy sports activities. Obviously you need some knowledge of your chosen sport or activity but basic knowledge, coupled with the ability to communicate effectively with the children, is often of more value than advanced knowledge alone.

Here are some ideas to consider – they are all skills which can easily be learned:

- You need a working knowledge of the techniques, skills and strategies of your sport, or to be prepared to learn about them. This you can find out from the sports governing body or other sport programmes developed for children[1].

- You must understand what is appropriate for the age and experience of the children participating (Section 6 Page 19 and Appendix B Page 33 will help).

- If you are going to be in charge, you need the ability to plan and organise sessions effectively. These must be geared to meet the children's specific needs – not simply a watered-down version of an adult session (Sections 4 and 7 Pages 13 and 23).

- Children should be protected. A knowledge of safety procedures and precautions appropriate to your activity is essential. Safety is always important but especially where children are involved (Section 3 Page 5).

- You need the knack of getting on the children's wavelength. Ideas should be explained clearly and concisely in simple language (Sections 4 and 6 Pages 13 and 19).

The rest of this pack will offer guidelines on how to develop these skills and put the ideas into practice.

1   The TOP Play and BT TOP Sport programmes provide sports coaches and some training to help deliver sports activities to children.

Even if you are just helping out for the first time, having children in your charge is a great responsibility. While they are with you, you are their guardian and must be responsible for their well-being. If you use your common sense and take the necessary precautions, you can minimise accidents and injuries. Forewarned is forearmed.

LEARN ABOUT YOUR SPORT

You must be aware of all the dangers inherent in the sport in which you are involved. In games, this means ensuring that everyone plays within the rules of the game – taking risks and using foul play can lead to injuries.

You are responsible for their well-being

EXAMPLE SAFETY POINTS FOR SMALL-SIDED BALL GAMES

Organisers should:

- use grids or ensure enough space is left between groups
- play to the rules
- match children carefully (physically and for ability) especially if contact is permitted
- use appropriate equipment (eg a lighter/softer ball, smaller/lower goals).

Organisers should ensure children:

- play sensibly – do not allow rough play
- challenge for the ball sensibly
- keep the ball under control (eg roll the ball back)
- take care when collecting balls or waiting for a turn
- move into a space – encourage children to look where they are going
- don't leave equipment lying around.

In other sports (eg swimming, athletics, gymnastics), it may be necessary to explain the potential dangers of the activity and establish certain rules about how to take part safely and what to do in an emergency (an example is provided in the panel below).

EXAMPLE SAFETY POINTS AT A SWIMMING POOL

Children should:

- not run or fool around on the pool-side

- not jump or dive into the water unless explicitly instructed to do so

- never play around in the water (eg push another swimmer under the water, throw floats, splash or create waves)

- stop immediately, swim to the side and await further instructions in silence if a whistle (or similar alarm) is sounded.

INSURANCE

Insurance cover for public liability and personal accident is essential for all helpers. Some sport governing bodies will not allow you to take part without such cover. Do not be put off – you will often find you are automatically covered by the body that organises your sport. Always check[1].

FIRST AID

You should always carry a small first aid kit to deal with minor injuries where they happen.

Wherever you are helping – at a local club, leisure centre or anywhere else where sport takes place – you should know where to find the medical kit and the nearest available phone in case of an emergency. As you become more involved, you should consider going on a first aid course[2] so you are prepared for emergencies. Some very basic guidelines are provided.

BASIC FIRST AID

- Dressings for wounds and grazes.
- Disposable gloves.
- Antiseptic solution.
- Clean water.
- Bandages/strapping.
- Scissors and safety pins.
- Ice or reusable ice packs.
- An eye pad.

---

1 If you are a qualified coach, you will be able to obtain insurance through membership of the National Association of Sports Coaches (Section 9 Page 30).

2 You may also wish to attend the key course *Prevention and Treatment of Injury* (details from your nearest NCF Regional Office, Page 30) or purchase the following handbook:
National Coaching Foundation (1995) *Sports injury: prevention and first aid management.* Revised edition. Leeds, National Coaching Foundation, Scottish Sports Council and St Andrews Ambulance Association. ISBN 1-850-168-2.

If there is an injury, STOP:

S *top* the activity and stay calm.

T *alk* to the injured child – reassure, ask what happened and if there is any pain.

O *bserve* while speaking – is behaviour normal or confused? Is any part misshapen or swollen? Any concerns – get help.

P *revent* further injury and decide if:

- severe injury is suspected, do not move and get professional help
- able to move without further injury, use RICED (see panel)
- very minor injury (eg bump, bruise), continue with activity but watch carefully.

If there is bleeding:

- cover wound with clean pad and apply hand pressure (wear disposable gloves if possible) press edges of wound together
- to the nose, sit the child down with head forward, loosen tight clothing and encourage to breathe through the mouth.

If bleeding is profuse:

- lay injured child down (keep head low) and raise bleeding area as high above the chest as possible (except for nose bleeds)
- prevent movement
- add further padding (do not remove first pad)

Use RICED:

R *est* – avoid activity.

I *ce* – keep injured part cold (use ice pack or cold water for no more than ten minutes, repeat frequently) and avoid heat (eg no hot bath, shower on injured part).

C *ompress* – strap the injured part to avoid swelling.

E *levate* the injured part (eg rest leg on chair).

D *octor* for full diagnosis.

- get medical help
- avoid direct contact with blood and wash hands as soon as possible.

HANDLING AN EMERGENCY

It is easy to panic when confronted with an injured child. Your first responsibility is to keep calm and phone for emergency help.

Once you know that help is on the way, the best treatment is usually to do nothing except keep the casualty warm and still. Never move the child if a serious injury is suspected – unless you must to avoid greater risk. Obviously, if there is severe bleeding, you should control it by applying pressure to the wound. In extreme circumstances, if breathing has stopped and there is no one at hand to help, you may need to attempt mouth-to-mouth resuscitation without delay – another reason why you should attend a first aid course.

MAKING THE ENVIRONMENT SAFE

It is your responsibility to ensure the facilities, equipment and surfaces are safe for the activity you are going to offer.

FACILITIES

Whether your sport takes place indoors or outdoors, always check the facilities before you start. Many buildings have been converted from other uses and are not always ideal. Typical examples of dangers are:

- indoors – protruding radiators not covered
- outdoors – broken glass or large stones on the ground.

EQUIPMENT

Equipment should be checked and maintained regularly. Tell the relevant authorities if anything needs mending or replacing – do not try to modify equipment yourself without expert guidance. Remember to keep the age and size of the children in mind when you select equipment to be used.

Match equipment to the child

SURFACES

Different sports use different types of surfaces, some natural and some synthetic. Although synthetic surfaces are very durable, they can cause friction burns when children fall, so keep your first aid kit properly stocked. To avoid unnecessary injury, ensure the children wear the appropriate footwear for the surface.

GENERAL GUIDANCE ON FOOTWEAR

Ensure footwear:

- fits firmly
- is flat-soled
- has sufficient grip for the surface (eg studs for soft ground or wet grass)
- will not damage the surface of the pitch, court or floor (eg black soled shoes mark wooden floors)

MAKING THE ACTIVITY SAFE

Having satisfied yourself that the facilities, clothing, footwear and equipment are safe, you must ensure the activities you include are appropriate for the children.

AT THE START

Some form of short, fun warm-up activity is recommended to prepare children physically and mentally for the forthcoming activity.

A suitable warm-up activity might include the following:

1 Start with some form of running game – starting at a slow pace and gradually increasing as the blood starts to circulate faster and the muscles and joints warm up.
For example: use three different coloured cards (eg traffic light colours) to indicate activity to be done. Show an amber coloured card and children jog slowly about the area; change to a red card and they stop and jump in the air; show both the red and amber cards and they jog with a high bouncy knee lift or a long stride; show the green card and they run fast with small controlled steps into a space.

2 Next a fun activity involving some gentle stretching and bending (eg of knees, ankles, arms – any parts which will be used later in the session). Discourage sudden or violent bending and stretching.
For example: children might be encouraged to reach out to draw a big circle slowly round their waist by reaching out in front and drawing an imaginary line right round to one side and then the other (with right hand and then the left); crouch down and do the same thing on the floor; then starting high above (and behind) their head, draw a big circle down to the floor and between their legs. Similar activities could be devised using a ball or passing an object from one child to another.

3 Finally a more vigorous activity – where possible related to the activity to follow or revising skills or games used in the last session.
For example: if a football type game is to be played, try a three child relay – each dribbles the ball up and round a marker and passes back to the next player.

Reach out to draw a circle slowly round the waist

It may also be possible to put each stage of the warm-up into one activity game. For example: mark out five activity stations (enough stations for 3–5 children to start at each one) and indicate the order in which they move from one to the next:

1 All children start by running lightly on the spot ten times, driving with their arms, then reach down to touch the floor and then up as high as possible (five times).

5 Children run to the next station, jump up high and touch the ground ten times. This may be repeated round one or more stations. NB Let them all do the same activity first time round (eg all do Activity 1 at whichever station they start, then second time do a different activity at each stage).

2 All the children in the group skip to the next station, clap hands ten times – once above their heads, then down by their feet, then to the left, then to the right, next behind their back (and repeat).

4 Each child runs backwards to the next station, looking carefully over the shoulder to avoid bumping into another child; here they stand back to back with a partner and pass an object (eg bean bag, ball) between them by twisting at the waist first to the left, then right, then over the head, between the legs and back over the head (and repeat).

3 All the children in the group take long strides (walking or leaping) to the next station where they jog on the spot and lift their knees as high as possible, using a vigorous arm action.

DURING THE SESSION

While you are helping out, ensure the children practise their skills and techniques safely:

- Make sure the techniques are appropriate for the age and experience of the children.

- Remember they are not mini adults – their minds and bodies are still developing.

- Group children according to age, height, skill or physical maturity as appropriate. Remember that children of the same age may be several years apart in physical development, so be fair.

- Keep an eye on the children's progress. You will often have to practise some stages of an activity several times and repeat something you did with them last week. Be patient and let children learn at their own pace.

- Keep a lookout for anyone looking tired or ill – that way you may avoid accidents and keep children from becoming discouraged.

- If it is hot, encourage children to drink regularly – they tend to dehydrate more quickly than adults. Don't wait until they are thirsty.

- If a child is injured, he/she should not continue. It may appear brave to limp on but this is not sensible and can cause further damage.

- Always maintain discipline. Fooling around can cause injuries. Make sure you model the behaviour you expect from the children.

- Keep activity times quite short. Base the duration and the scheduling of practices and competitions on the age, capability and maturity of the children.

FINISHING THE SESSION

It is useful to cool down after exercise as well as warm up beforehand. Choose a slower pace activity to calm the children, give the body a chance to recover and reduce the likelihood of muscle stiffness. Ensure they put on extra clothing to avoid getting cold.

CHILDREN FIRST

First and foremost sport should be fun so it is important to place the well-being and interests of the children above everything else. If you follow this advice, you will not go far wrong.

- Children first, winning second. Too much emphasis is often placed simply on winning rather than on effort or improvement. Those who lose – the majority – are too often wrongly regarded as failures.

- Avoid giving extra attention and playing time to the more talented children. Average and less talented children need and deserve equal time. Be sensitive to those who are less talented.

- Be reasonable in your demands on young people's time, energy and enthusiasm – children need other interests. For some, sport may not be their greatest interest and you should accept this.

- Always follow the advice of a doctor when deciding when an injured child is ready to take part again.

- Encourage and develop respect for the abilities of opponents, as well as for the judgement of officials and opposing helpers. Develop a sense of fair play and the importance of doing your best.

THINK SAFE

Sport should be fun and children should be and feel safe. As a parent, coach or leader, you have a responsibility to do everything you can to protect children from all forms of abuse (Page 31). It is not up to you to decide whether or not abuse is taking place but it is your responsibility to act if you are concerned. You should ensure that children also know what to do if they are concerned[1].

If you are concerned about a child, talk to:

- the parents or carers first – unless you are concerned about sexual abuse or violence at home

- someone you can trust – the person in charge of the session or the venue

- the Social Services or the Police.

OR phone the NSPCC Helpline on 0800 800 500.

SUMMARY

Remember you must ensure children's safety by:

- thinking safe – always check facilities, equipment and surfaces and ensure the activity is appropriate for the developmental age and ability of the child

- putting the welfare of the child first

- acting on any concern you may have about the welfare of the child

- knowing about first aid and how to cope in an emergency.

---

1   Children's posters are included in every TOP Play and TOP Sport bag. Also check if they are available from your sport or local authority.

Your contribution to the children's enjoyment will be much greater if you take the trouble to plan in advance and organise yourself and the children. Many of the problems you may have when you first start helping may have nothing to do with personality, control or knowledge – they are probably due simply to a lack of preparation and organisation.

PLANNING

Planning need not be elaborate – just a little forethought before the session will make all the difference:

- Find out the ability, previous experience and interests of the children.

- Decide what you want to achieve with the children – be challenging but not too ambitious.

- Always keep in mind the age and developmental stage of the child.

- Always think about the possible danger areas. Anticipate problems – think safe.

- Plan in advance how you will divide the children into groups or teams (eg by size/ability or their choice).

- Allow a little time for the warm-up and cool-down but ensure most of the time is allocated to the main activity.

- Keep activities varied but simple. Do not include too many new activities – children can only take in so much. One thing learned well is better than several learned badly.

- Ask experienced coaches for advice on planning.

Keep in mind the developmental stage of each child

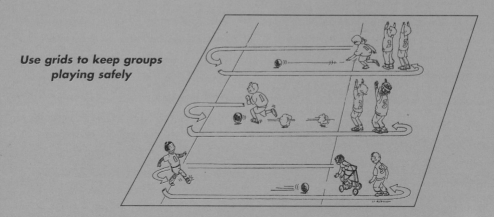

Use grids to keep groups playing safely

ORGANISATION

Good organisation during the session saves time, encourages attention and discipline, maintains safety, and maximises the opportunities for activity and fun. A few guidelines can help:

- Ensure you gain the children's attention and that everyone can see and hear you before you give instructions (eg check children are not distracted by other activities, make sure you have the sun in your eyes, not the children's).

- Work out in advance how you will group children. It may help to call children into a semicircle – you can see everyone and they can see you; instructions and demonstrations are therefore easy. When building from pairs or threes into larger groups, try to work up in multiples (eg 2s to 4s, 3s to 6s).

- Give simple clear instructions such as:
  - stand with a partner about your size

  - join up with another pair
  - one ball between three
  - number yourselves A and B – A collects a ball while B fetches a bat.

- Mark out playing areas before the session. It may help to use grids which can be any size and easily marked. Grids can be marked by cones, ropes or bean bags, as well as by drawing chalk lines. Grids may help to keep a group together ensuring control and safety, and avoiding distractions.

SUMMARY

- Fail to plan, plan to fail.
- Spend time thinking through exactly what you will do and how you will do it before the session.
- Keep things simple – clear instructions and tasks, easily understood rules, build activities up slowly.

Motivation begins with you. If you have no enthusiasm and little interest, any motivation the youngsters have will soon disappear.

WHY ARE THEY HERE?

Before working with any group, ask yourself – have they come because:

- they simply enjoy the sport
- they like being with others
- they want to improve their skills
- their parents want them to be there?

The answer is probably a mixture of all of these reasons but be sure you are working to help children achieve their goals – not their parents and certainly not yours.

WHAT IS MOTIVATION?

Many different factors motivate children to take part in sport. Enthusiastic children are motivated by the:

- enjoyment of taking part
- sense of involvement with a group
- pleasure of improving their own performance
- reward gained from performing well.

Excessive external pressures from helpers, coaches, parents and others may prove counter-productive. Enthusiastic and successful children are self-motivated – they are there because they want to be there, not because you or anyone else wants them to take part.

Children are motivated when they experience some success

YOUR CONTRIBUTION

There are different ways of motivating children effectively. Whether you are a live wire or the quiet but firm type, children will react well to the genuine enthusiasm you bring to your session, rather than to a brash approach. The following guidelines may help:

- Honest words of praise are very effective tools. Naturally, the encouragement you give must be finely tuned to get the best out of each youngster. Some children respond well to frequent praise, others may stop trying so hard.

- Recognise the difficulties and pressures which children face, both in and out of sport. These can include overambitious parents, shyness, worry about examinations, even concern about you. Try to identify problems early and talk about them in a sympathetic manner.

- Children quickly learn that sport involves competition with others. Keep winning in perspective – the idea that coming first is all that matters can result in great disappointment and disillusionment. Try to create a positive atmosphere, where effort and progress are just as important as winning. Encourage the children to improve their personal bests, achieve moves they have not done before or simply to be wholehearted in their involvement.

Children respond to the general enthusiasm you bring

COPING WITH PRESSURE

Pressures in sport come in a variety of forms (eg trying too hard, wanting to win or more often not wanting to lose, excessive expectations of parents, friends or even the leaders and coaches).

Each child is an individual and will show the effects of pressure in different ways. Some become loud and talkative, while others withdraw into themselves. Whatever the cause, remember that a certain amount of stress can help produce a peak performance – but too much is destructive. Excessive pressure will make the children feel threatened and the resulting anxiety will make it difficult for them to cope.

Be sensitive to children's anxiety levels. If they are overanxious, make a special effort to help them cope. Stay calm yourself and help them focus on the positive side of the situation. Above all, be supportive.

WORKING TOGETHER

Some form of very simple target or goal-setting can be valuable – it helps to focus attention and confirm progress and success. A simple goal should be set for each session – it might be about improving a particular skill, helping a partner, playing as a team. Children should also be encouraged to set their own goals based on their own performance rather than on whether or not they win. This way, success is measured in terms of things such as effort and team co-operation. These are achievements over which the child has some control.

GOOD GOAL-SETTING

Set simple goals with young children – improving a personal best, helping a partner, playing to the rules.

- Success is vital. Modify the goal if necessary to ensure it offers every child some challenge but also a real chance of achieving some success.

- Avoid goals which are only about winning or which depend on others for success.

- Share the goal with the child. Remember to comment on progress and praise achievement and effort.

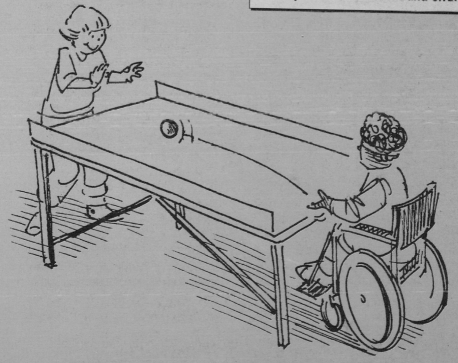

Modify the goal to ensure everyone achieves some success

SAFEGUARDING VALUES

Working with children brings special responsibilities. The inappropriate expectations and attitudes of adults can jeopardise children's enjoyment and will influence their attitude towards sport and fair play. You have an opportunity to promote fair play in sport through encouraging participation, teamwork and an appreciation of the spirit of the game.

Parents can promote the positive side of sport by:

- not forcing an unwilling child to participate – children should not take part to fulfil their parents' ambitions
- encouraging their children to play to the rules and show respect for the opposition, the officials and the coach
- rewarding effort and improvement rather than only winning
- setting a good example on and off the field of play (NB spectating parents can become over-involved in supporting their child and team, and shout criticisms to the opposition, official and coach).

Leaders and coaches can help by:

- ensuring effort, skill improvement and fair play are each rewarded by praise
- explaining the differences between children's sport and professional sport – professionals are entertainers and wage earners and as such their behaviour may be different

- placing the needs and interests of each child above those of the sport or the team
- ensuring the children know and abide by the rules of the sport or game
- encouraging children to respect the opponents, the officials and other coaches
- setting a good example outside the sports arena as well as on the field, court or track, in the gym or pool.

Officials in games can help by:

- using common sense to ensure the spirit of the game or activity is not lost (eg by overuse of the whistle)
- being consistent, objective and courteous in dealing with rule infringements and fouls
- condemning gamesmanship (eg professional fouls) and praising fair play.

SUMMARY

Keep sport fun and fair:

- Know what motivates each child to take part.
- Be supportive.
- Keep winning in perspective – use praise to reward effort and achievement.
- Promote fair play – demand and demonstrate respect for opponents, officials and coaches.

As you learn more about sport and become more confident with the children, you will probably find that you slide effortlessly into the role of teacher or coach. It will help if you have some knowledge of effective teaching and coaching techniques and know when to introduce skills, tactics and rules.

WHAT TO TEACH

Before you start, assess the ability level of the children and give careful consideration to their age and physical build. Some sports are simply not suitable for young children, so you need to take account of physical development at all stages.

Before you start, assess the child's ability

Guidelines for determining content:

- The better you understand the techniques, skills and tactics of your particular sport, the more effectively you will be able to pass this knowledge on to others.

- Start with the basics. Try to ensure a gradual build-up of skill and be patient – children need time. Often your greatest need will be patience.

- Introducing tactics and strategies has to be done very carefully. For example, young players may not readily understand positional play. Keep it simple – what appears obvious and straightforward to you, may be hard for newcomers to master.

- The adult or elite form of the sport is unlikely to be appropriate for young or novice players. You should always change the form of the game or sport to fit the children. Typical examples are:

  - mini-rugby, where contact is kept to a minimum
  - mini-volleyball, which uses a smaller court and fewer players
  - short tennis, with its small court, adapted rackets and sponge balls.

When modified sports are used, the children will have:

- more opportunities (eg smaller sided games give greater opportunities for kicking, hitting or passing the ball)
- more fun
- better skill development[1].

WAYS TO MODIFY

- Adapt rules.
- Reduce playing time.
- Reduce equipment size.
- Reduce the size of the playing area.
- Provide more protection from injury.
- Use adapted equipment (eg softer or smaller ball).

HOW TO TEACH

Keep children active – they learn best by doing. They will soon become bored listening to you give lengthy explanations.

Don't keep them waiting in queues to do the activity – that will only teach them to queue. It is best to keep the number of children in an activity as few as possible – that way each child has more turns, more time to practise and more fun. Try to keep practices as game-like as possible, and explain why you have selected particular activities.

Train your eye so you can observe and analyse individuals in action. At each stage, try to focus your attention on one or two particular aspects of the technique (eg footwork, racket grip, position of the head or hand).

Try to give equal time to all the children, regardless of ability.

Children learn by doing not by queueing

1   There are a number of good activity cards on the market that use modified game forms (eg TOP Play, BT TOP Sport cards).

SEVEN STEPS TO SUCCESS

Try this way of teaching the children a new activity:

- Let them have a go – explain the task clearly and simply, then stand back and observe.
- Demonstrate the action a couple of times with minimum explanation.
- Allow them to practise and observe them carefully.
- Provide feedback while the practice continues, by moving round the group and giving extra help to those who need it.
- If necessary, stop the practice to reinforce a point made earlier, or to analyse general problems the group is encountering.
- Encourage further practice to produce improvements. Remember to provide some variety.
- Give plenty of praise – try to build on what they are doing right rather than tell them what they are doing wrong.

Provide feedback while they practise

Don't make children afraid to make mistakes

HOW TO ENCOURAGE LEARNING

Enthusiasm works wonders. If you can communicate your enthusiasm, the children will be eager to learn and will get real enjoyment from their sport. Keep it positive:

- Look for things to praise – particularly in children who might not otherwise gain attention.
- Beginners need plenty of praise and encouragement. However, once they have developed their skills, praise will be effective if used more judiciously.
- Praise good behaviour at once – show you value it.

- Praise effort and performance more than results. A skilful shot at goal is still good even if the goalie saves it; a fast time is still good even if the child does not win.
- Remember, children don't generally make mistakes on purpose; help them to learn from their mistakes when they do crop up.
- Accept mistakes as part of learning. Don't make children afraid to fail or make mistakes – they will stop trying and stop learning. Adjust the training to avoid repeated mistakes.
- Avoid sarcasm and shouting at the children. It sets a very bad example and is both humiliating and discouraging.

SUMMARY

Remember when starting to teach to:
- build up the activity or skill gradually
- use modified game forms whenever possible
- keep the number of children in the team or group as small as possible
- use the seven steps to success
- encourage learning by praising effort and improvement
- accept mistakes as an essential part of learning.

What would happen if the usual organiser of the group asked you to handle the next couple of sessions because he/she was going away on business or the coach was rushed into hospital? Using the guidelines in this pack, you should be able to move from being a casual helper to being a skilled helper who can manage sessions safely and effectively. The importance of planning has already been mentioned (Section 4 Page 13).

PLANNING

- Decide the goal for the session and plan the activities to meet the goal.

- Ensure the goal you set is challenging but achievable and appropriate to the developmental stage and ability of the children.

- Plan out the content – how you will start the session, how the activities will progress, how you will end the session. A session planner (see example on Page 24) will help you to do this. Check out the content with a coach. If this is not possible, use content you have used before or stick to activity cards.

- Plan the organisation of the session – the equipment, the children and the timing.

STARTING

- One thing you can always do is start on time. You should arrive at the session well ahead of the start time to check the facilities and prepare the equipment before your group arrives. Encourage the children to arrive early and to be changed ready to start on the dot.

- Make the first activity fun. Latecomers will have to wait a little to join in and this will encourage everyone to be ready next time.

- Remember to include a warm-up activity before moving into other practices or more vigorous activities (refer back to Pages 9–10).

- Explain clearly what you are hoping to do in the session (the goals) and why.

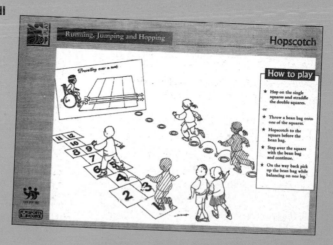

If in doubt, use activity cards

DATE: 3 March	VENUE: Hall
EQUIPMENT REQUIRED: 20 tennis balls	GROUP: 20 eight year olds (mixed)

GOALS/OBJECTIVES: Develop skills of ball throwing, catching and bouncing

ORGANISATION/PRESENTATION	COACHING POINTS
WARM-UP/INTRODUCTION (10 mins) 1 In 2s, A holds tennis ball, B sets off at fast walking pace, after 5 strides. A follows. A tries to catch B and place ball gently on B's back. Change over, repeat, jogging instead of walking. Change again, leader runs faster. 2 'Stop', partners stand arms length apart, stretch to pass ball at waist height, by feet, then overhead and between legs. Repeat Steps 1 and 2.	Leader must run into spaces and not bump into anyone. May not throw ball. Encourage to stretch as far as possible.

MAIN CONTENT (30 mins)
1 One ball each, practise last week's activities:
   – Roll ball forward short distance, chase and pick up
   – Dribble ball with feet, keeping ball no more than 1 foot away
   – Bounce and catch (first static and then moving)
   – Toss up and catch (first static and then moving).
 	
2 In grid in 2s, stand 2 metres apart, easy underarm throw to partner to catch. Count number of catches in one minute. Catcher chooses height to receive ball – high, low, left, right, then catcher moves to catch. Count number of catches in one minute. Add bounce pass – ensuring bounces to correct height.
 	
3 Join up with two from next grid, one pair throw and catch, one of the second pair (pig) tries to intercept ball, fourth child is scorer. Pig gets one point if touches ball, or if the ball is held more than 5 seconds, 3 points if intercepts. Change round (after 3 points/2 minutes).
 	
4 Choose one group for demonstration – ask:
   How clearly does catcher show where wants ball?
   Where might pig stand – near thrower, near catcher?
   Help children with simple tactics (eg height of throw, distance of pass, position of pig, use of bounce pass – where should it bounce? Back into groups – one more turn each as pig, count points scored in 3 minutes.
   If time, introduce overarm throw to more skilled groups.
	Roll gently, no bounce, bend low. Keep ball close. Gentle, don't slap ball, soft hands. Watch ball, give as catch (soft, silent).
	
	Smooth arm and wrist in throwing, follow through towards parner's hands. Watch ball as catch, hands together, soft and give.
	
	Catcher chooses where to ask for ball according to position of the pig. Scorer's opinion is final.

COOL-DOWN/SUMMARY (5 mins)
Four players in a train – leader holds the ball, decides direction and pace; on whistle, change the engine and ball given to next player/carriage who becomes engine, engine player to guard's van. At each change, train moves more slowly until it finally stops. Ask for scores and praise all as appropriate.

DURING THE SESSION

During the session, be firm in your control and organisation of the group.

STOPPING A GROUP

Never stop the group until you know what you are going to say. Avoid stopping the activity unless you have something valuable to say. Stop everyone from a position where you are clearly visible and can direct your voice to all of them.

USING YOUR VOICE

- Be clear but never aggressive. It is not only *what* is said but also *how* it is said, that matters.
- Remember, don't talk too much or they will stop listening. Children are there to take part and have fun.
- Use plenty of praise and encouragement while the group is working.
- Direct your comments to the furthest child (without shouting) as well as the nearest.
- Check you can be heard by the whole group.

Where comments or instructions are brief, there is no need to bring the group together. However, if something requires more detailed explanation, you should gather the group in closer or wait until the end of the activity.

DEMONSTRATION

Demonstration is far better than explanation – as long as it is appropriate:

- Make sure the demonstration is simple enough for a child to repeat and practise. Don't show off – where possible use a child to demonstrate.
- Don't pick more than one point to demonstrate at a time – guide the children's attention to the most important things (eg watch his feet, look at her hand).
- Repeat the demonstration at least twice.
- Let them try it for themselves and allow plenty of time to try out each new skill.

WORKING IN GROUPS

Many activities are best practised in small groups. The best group size depends on the activity. The key is to involve everyone as fully as possible. Remember:

- by keeping groups small, everyone has a better chance to master the skills and learn the rules of team games
- if you increase the group size, select numbers that allow an easy progression, such as 3 vs 3 up to 6 vs 6, and 2 vs 2 up to 4 vs 4.

ENDING THE SESSION

- Always finish on time – someone else may want to use the equipment after you and the children may have somewhere else to go. Remember the cool-down activity to calm them down. Bring the group in and ask them how they feel they have done, whether they achieved the goals set. Praise them for their effort and achievement as appropriate.

- Involve everyone in collecting all the equipment and clearing the facilities. Don't end up putting everything away yourself.

- Give the children any instructions about the next session or competition.

- Finish on an optimistic note with a word of encouragement or you may find the group is smaller at the next practice session.

AFTER THE SESSION

As soon as possible after the session, make notes on the planner about how everything went. Try to assess what:

- went well

- went badly

- is needed for next time.

Make a note for the next session to remind you about any areas that need further work.

SUMMARY

Remember when running a session to:

- use the session planner beforehand to map out content and organisation thoroughly

- check the facility and equipment for safety before the start (refer back to Page 8)

- make the start and warm-up activity fun

- keep control of the group through good organisation and effective use of the voice

- make the activities fun and ensure simple progressions from one to another

- leave time to finish the session properly

- assess how well the session went and use what you have learned in planning and running subsequent sessions

- consider embarking on a coaching course to develop your knowledge and skills (further details on Page 30).

Children's physical fitness is almost certain to improve just by taking part in sport – it is easy for over-enthusiastic helpers and coaches to concentrate too much on fitness training. Few youngsters need the sort of training regime that produces championship-winning performances and most will soon become bored if you try to inflict such regimes on them.

All children should do some warm-up activities before the more vigorous activity starts (Pages 9–10). A little general fitness training may also be introduced. This will usually be enough, at least until they are entering their teens. When more serious and specific training becomes appropriate, you may include more formal fitness work. Use the following guidelines.

PHYSICAL FITNESS

Physical fitness involves the overall physical condition of the individual. It includes endurance, strength, speed and flexibility.

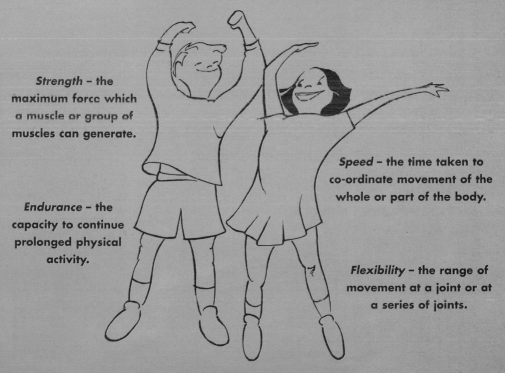

Strength – the maximum force which a muscle or group of muscles can generate.

Endurance – the capacity to continue prolonged physical activity.

Speed – the time taken to co-ordinate movement of the whole or part of the body.

Flexibility – the range of movement at a joint or at a series of joints.

Components of fitness

THINK ABOUT EACH CHILD

Each child is unique and will respond differently to the same training. Before devising programmes, bear in mind that your sessions are probably not the only physical activity in which the children may be involved. You need to find out what else they are doing before you can devise a sensible level of training. The best way to do this is to encourage the youngsters to keep a note in a diary of all the physical activity they do – in school time as well as in after-school activities and clubs. If they go on into really serious sport, this will also have the benefit of establishing a good habit at an early age.

Regardless of the training you devise and the enthusiasm of the children, always build up slowly. If you increase training too quickly, the young bodies will not be able to adapt to it and this may result in injury. Never push children to extremes.

MAKE FITNESS-TRAINING FUN

Children have short attention spans and easily get bored, so vary the activities to keep fitness training fun.

- Try to plan your fitness sessions and keep a record of them, so you know you are providing variety.

- Listen to the children and try to use their ideas as well as your own.

- Leave physical conditioning sessions until after skills work.

- Explain to the group why they are doing particular exercises.

- Set realistic targets for each child to reach and always give plenty of praise and encouragement for effort as well as achievement.

- Never use fitness training as a punishment as this will discourage them from enjoying it.

TYPES OF TRAINING

There are a number of different types of training and each has its own purpose and place.

RUNNING

Running in its various forms is an important aspect of training. Vary what you do because jogging round the playing fields or gym can get very tedious. Shuttle runs, longer runs with a change of pace, or team runs where each member must finish before the team is home, all provide variety. Above all, be imaginative and make sure the type of running relates to the demands of the sport.

CIRCUIT TRAINING

Circuit training consists of a series of exercises designed to work different sets of muscles. The circuit of exercises is usually done against the clock and is a good form of endurance training. Devising a circuit is a skilled job, so seek advice from more experienced coaches about which exercises to use and the correct way of doing them. Remember that damage can be caused through incorrect exercise, particularly with young people.

WEIGHT TRAINING

Weight training can have a harmful effect on growth, so children and young people should not normally use it until their bone development is complete. This is usually after puberty but remember that the age at which puberty finishes can vary considerably.

Children should only use their own body weight in strength exercises. Even with older children and young adults, always seek expert advice before introducing weight training.

FOOD AND REST

A healthy diet is essential if young growing bodies are to keep fit and develop properly. Make sure children do not skip meals to come to training. One or two meals missed may not be a problem but regular poor eating will result in fatigue and possible injury. Use your influence to encourage the children to eat a balanced diet, with a good mixture of foods, and ensure they drink plenty of fluids, especially in warm weather. Drinks should be available both during and after exercise.

Rest is also important, particularly for younger children. Make sure they have some complete rest days and encourage them to go to bed early.

Drinks should always be available

SUMMARY

Fitness is an essential part of peak performance in all sports. It should be introduced carefully and sensibly, providing a sound basis on which to build. Regular and sustained progress is the objective.

Many helpers find they enjoy their involvement with children in sport so much they wish to learn more. If you want to develop your skills further, there are a number of ways and places to help you:

Contact *the National Coaching Foundation* for details about:

- courses for coaches at all levels on different topics (eg fitness, injury prevention, motivation)
- insurance through membership of the National Association of Sports Coaches (Page 6):

The National Coaching Foundation
114 Cardigan Road
Headingley
Leeds LS6 3BJ
Telephone: 0113 274 4802
Fax: 0113 275 5019.

The NCF has regional offices in every part of England and equivalent coaching centres in Scotland, Wales and Northern Ireland. Telephone numbers are given in the NCF's regular bulletin, *Supercoach* – available free from the NCF in Leeds.

Contact *Coachwise* for a catalogue about the books and videos available on all aspects of sports coaching:

Telephone: 0113 231 1310
Fax: 0113 231 9606.

Contact *the Youth Sport Trust* for more information on TOP programmes:

The Youth Sport Trust
Rutland Building
Loughborough University of Technology
Loughborough LE11 3TU
Tel: 01509 228293
Fax: 01509 210851.

Contact the *Central Council of Physical Recreation* for the address of your sport's national governing body:

The Central Council of Physical Recreation
Francis House
Francis Street
London SW1P 1DE
Telephone: 0171 828 3163
Fax: 0171 630 8820.

Contact the *Sports Council* to find out what is happening in your area:

The English Sports Council
Telephone: 0171 273 1500.

The Scottish Sports Council
Telephone: 0131 317 7200.

The Sports Council for Northern Ireland
Telephone: 01232 381222.

The Sports Council for Wales
Telephone: 01222 397571.

Contact the *National Play Information Centre* for information on all issues related to children's play:

The National Play Information Centre
First Floor
359–361 Euston Road
London NW1 3AL
Telephone: 0171 383 5455
Fax: 0171 387 3152.

Child abuse is a term used to describe ways in which children are harmed, usually by adults and often by people they know and trust. It refers to the damage done to a child's physical or mental health. Children can be abused within or outside their family, at school and even in the sports environment. Child abuse can take many forms:

Physical abuse, where adults:

- physically hurt or injure children (eg by hitting, shaking, squeezing, biting or burning)
- give children alcohol, inappropriate drugs or poison
- attempt to suffocate or drown children.

In sport situations, physical abuse might occur when the nature and intensity of training exceeds the capacity of the child's immature and growing body.

Neglect includes situations in which adults:

- fail to meet a child's basic physical needs (eg for food, warm clothing)
- consistently leave children alone and unsupervised
- fail or refuse to give children love, affection or attention.

Neglect in a sports situation might occur if a teacher or coach fails to ensure children are safe or exposes them to undue cold or risk of injury.

Emotional abuse can occur in a number of ways. For example, where:

- there is persistent lack of love or affection
- there is constant overprotection which prevents children from socialising
- children are constantly being shouted at or taunted
- there is neglect, physical or sexual abuse.

Emotional abuse in sport might include situations where parents or coaches subject children to constant criticism, bullying or unrealistic pressure to perform to high expectations.

Sexual abuse. Boys and girls are sexually abused when adults (male and female) use them to meet their own sexual needs. This could include:

- full sexual intercourse, masturbation, oral sex, fondling
- showing children pornographic books, photographs or videos, or taking pictures for pornographic purposes.

Sport situations which involve physical contact (eg supporting or guiding children) could potentially create situations where sexual abuse may go unnoticed. Abusive situations may also occur if adults misuse their power over young people.

WHAT IF I HAVE CONCERNS?

1 If you have noticed a change in the child's behaviour, first talk to the parents or carers. It may be that something has happened, perhaps a bereavement, which has caused the child to be unhappy. However, if your concerns are about sexual abuse or violence, talking to the parents or carers might put the child at greater risk.

2 If your concerns remain or you cannot talk to the parents/carers, consult the person in charge or someone you can trust. It is the responsibility of the person in charge to make the decision to contact Social Services.

3 If the person in charge is not available, the concerns are about him/her, or you do not feel appropriate action has been taken, you must contact Social Services or the Police yourself. The number is in the phone book. If you want to talk things through to obtain some advice, you can phone the NSPCC free HelpLine on 0800 800 500. This operates 24 hours a day, every day. You do not have to give your name but it is helpful if you can.